THE DOOR TO COLOUR

Myra Schneider

THE DOOR TO
COLOUR

ENITHARMON PRESS

First published in 2014
by Enitharmon Press
10 Bury Place
London WC1A 2JL

www.enitharmon.co.uk

Distributed in the UK by
Central Books
99 Wallis Road
London E9 5LN

ISBN: 978-1-907587-51-1

Enitharmon Press gratefully acknowledges the financial support of
Arts Council England through Grants for the Arts.

British Library Cataloguing-in-Publication Data.
A catalogue record for this book is available
from the British Library.

Designed in Albertina by Libanus Press
and printed in England by SRP

CONTENTS

LE CITRON

after Manet

Day after day I contemplate this lemon,
the small weightiness of its rounded body
bedded on a plate whose mood is olive. Its tang
is sharp as frostnip yet not hostile,
its skin landscaped with yellows that sing
in counterpoint to mustard and leaf green.
When I journey to the points at each pole
I'm touched by their vulnerability.
At dusk the plate's faintly rimmed with silver
as if dreaming it's moonshine and the lemon
swells to a globe which illuminates a room
yearning for furniture, flowered curtains,
the comfort of carpet. I can hardly bear
to see it in such isolated splendour.

IT'S POSSIBLE

when you scrutinize a sycamore's fists
and find its green thoughts
are not ready to uncrumple,

when you finger the kitchen tulips
whose pouts are now pink beaks,
see speckled song in the tigerlily throats,

when you peel a blood orange
and eat the ruby segments
while gazing at Himalayas of cloud

whiter than ice cream, at the sky
beyond them, its untouchable blue
which science explains but you feel

belongs to ever – it's possible
you'll believe that at the moment
darkness first split to let in light

some kind of consciousness
must have emerged and created
the multiplicity of colour.

KALEIDOSCOPE

Discovery

Some days mist wiped out the world that lay
below our house, days grey as the ash heaped
in the grate, thick as the lumpy nastiness
of porridge which syrup couldn't disguise.

Those days weighed on me like art at school:
drawing cylinders, cubes, heavy books on sheets
of off-white paper and not being allowed to touch
the boxes of crayons whose colours burned bright.

There was the day I knelt on the nursery lino,
picked up the kaleidoscope, peered into
its dark tube and gasped at the lime-green leafing
countless circles of purple petals, at the threading

of moon crescents to stars and dots of gold.
One shake and this vision vanished but another
arose and with every shake another. I could erase
and create magical worlds whenever I chose.

Red

is the leaves you try to catch
as they drop into winter, the flare
from the Halloween turnip's heart

that lights up its cut-out eyes,
the dooking for apples in water,
the solid prize you bite into.

Red prickles your fingers, spurts
from your knee the day you trip
with bottles of milk on the lid of a drain.

You develop a dread of red
even before it claws you with ache,
leaks from your body and soaks

through pads which you learn
to wrap up and dispose of in silence.
But you can't kill the smell of shame

and you hate red, the cunning
with which it's trapped you for life.
Yet there are days when red

becomes the possibility of wearing
a dress called excitement,
of nameless seeds spreading.

Floating

after Chagall

Standing hand in hand in this room
full of evening – surely it isn't a dream
that we've found one another? The windows
spring open as if aware we can't be held in.

Now we're out there's no keeping our feet
on the ground. Our hearts are overflowing
and look, we're above the street, floating
above the sleeping houses. We're so high

I could touch the moon's tip, stroke
the sky's lavenders and aquamarines
which are slowly giving birth to a violet
momentous as our feelings. You fold me

into your arms and I can think of nothing
more romantic than the way we're sailing
towards the massed singing that's emerging
from flowers in a forest of leaf and fern.

Oh look! there's a donkey far below
sitting on the peak of a roof – it's pricked up
its ears and perhaps is gazing at the blues
of our world. I think it can hear our happiness.

Circling

You can forget the bump into reality
when the colours lost their shine, forget
the blank months, the nothingness of streets,
the bittergrey which ate into your mind.
You have a partner now and a child,
are part of the party game. You all go
round and round, hands linked, revelling
in the movements of legs and arms.
The air reverberates with energy.
The sun comes out, turns your salmon skin
sand-orange. The laughter is amber.

The circling is getting faster – too fast.
'Stop!' you shout but your voice
is drowned by others bawling slogans.
You're on a roundabout that's out of control,
will be carried away if you don't jump.

The ground's full of cracks and potholes
but bracing yourself, you leap – land
on your knees. You're bruised but it's a relief
to return to the muted everyday, to relax
on the quiet paisley of your sofa, switch off
your mind, watch a black and white film.

His Room

On the door: posters, cuttings
and a warning: *Parents Keep Out.*
I knock, am admitted.

He's painted one wall apricot.
The ceiling is striped with rays
from an over-bright sun.

An ominous black dominates
the wall by the window. I'm careful
not to comment on the bicycle tyre

poking out from under the bed
or the waste-heap of books,
boots and unwashed clothing.

'I've got to find out if life
has any meaning,' he tells me.
He is fifteen, I am forty-five

and the meanings I thought I'd found
have vanished. But behind him
I see myself at fifteen overwhelmed

by black and orange, groping
for answers, not being heard.
Heart full, I listen, I sympathize.

Silence

is silver so you try to hoard it
in your small room among books,
folders, boxes topped with dust,
the dangle of computer cables.

The phone rings. You switch it off
but you can't settle to anything –
the walls, the floor and the air
are all infected with a whirr

you can't identify. Worse, the voices
in your head, which are always
on the lookout for a chance
to criticize, refuse to lie down.

'What colour is noise?' you ask.
There's no reply. You stare
at the screen for inspiration,
at last write: *Tranquillity is gold.*

Panic

I expect it to strike in a scarlet wild
as underskirts swirling in dance,
inflamed as my throat in the grip
of tonsilitis, furious as the bull
that materialized one afternoon
from nowhere in a field where fence
and hedge were far out of reach.

But when sleep refuses
in the pit of night panic is the cur
that never fails to sniff out opportunity.

One yap and its bad breath
is under the duvet, its teeth
sink into my neck, it stirs
havoc in my stomach. In seconds

it blows up like a balloon, sucks in
house and mouthfuls of garden, laughs
as an ambulance screeches disaster.
Not red, its apparel at night,
but a black which eclipses
streetlight and searchlight, a black
that out-dazzles equatorial sun.

Garden

Day has washed away the dark – road signs
and car bonnets are bathed in light. Go into
the garden where dandelions pit themselves
against primroses, and white flutters
of pear blossom settle on the unruly lawn –

or take yourself back to your first garden
where you stroked the furry lambs' ears
in the rockery, picked bobbles in the privet
for their sweet clothiness, ran away
from the temper of Mrs Goldie next door,

ashamed that she'd called you a little devil.
You knew you must have done something wrong
and for five minutes wondered what – hacking
a worm in two or biting into the crimson apple
your friend stole and invited you to taste?

No point now in trying to pinpoint your crime –
even if you managed to make your way back
you know you'd find the gate locked, know
rattling the handle wouldn't summon anyone
to swing it open. No way to re-enter that time.

The Pit

Is it because green is going to peter out
that I find myself in a field of bleached stalks?
I make my way to a river. Its bed is waterless,
covered with mud cracked as ancient skin.

When I walk on, sand blows into my hair. No birds
are singing in the puny trees. A prickly plant
that's determined to survive in this place
of broken stones, cuts sharply into my shin.

I lean over a cistern hewn into rock. It's edged
with shrivelled moss, its emptiness smells
of death. Millennia collapse: this could be the pit
Joseph was thrown into by his jealous brothers.

And although I press my palms against my eyes
I cannnot blot it out – that beautiful coat the boy
was given by his father. Its fabric is torn, its purples
and pinks are smeared with dirt, stained with blood.

Travelling

A city of calcified bones
and mouths roaring hunger
disappears when you notice

a minute green spider running
up your arm. You stop moping
on the settee, put on trainers,

pack a rucksack with necessities
and although you're well beyond
middle age, you set off.

After days, or maybe it's weeks
of travel, you come to a house
with Van Gogh-yellow walls

which seem to offer hope.
Inside there are airy panels
of quiet in the waiting room,

tension slips off your shoulders
easily as a coat and you sit patiently
with the others inside themselves.

The doctor writes you a prescription
which turns out to be a diagram
of the route you should take. At last

the heart-stopping moment
of light hovering on water and soon
you reach a lake that's been fed

by the blue above. You remember
your child once asked: 'What holds
the sky up so it doesn't fall down?'

The quayside beckons with a list
of excursions, you board a boat
that's about to sail to *The Island*.

The Butterfly House

As the glass door closes behind me
I'm immersed in the green of leafery and fern

and wherever I look butterflies flitter,
their wings wider than my palms, wings

with crimson panels on purple dusk,
dramatic with mosaics in black and white.

In this new dimension I'm smiling
as if I too were winged, almost weightless.

Entranced, I move among the flying flowers.
And I want to stay in this place so far beyond

my first garden, beyond the other edens
I've concocted, live in this temple devoted

to nurture. But it's closing time. An insect
with sapphire skirts is supping on an orange

laid out by hands, the air is belled with light.
Lightened, I slip back to the other world.

THE THROW

my son brought me from Thailand is magenta,
a royal marriage of violet and pink.
When I lay it on my bed over the quilt
from India it becomes an extra skin,
one that's kind to my uncomfortable body.

How I love its minute gold elephants, each
the size of the top segment of my little finger.
They walk in perfect lines, head to tail,
along the embroidered roads of the fabric
and when I stroke one an elephant god appears,

becomes the memory of riding in a high place
on a huge blur of animal, becomes the elephants
living in Mimi's flat. My son has elaborated
on the heat in Thailand but here winter is trying
to sneak into the house and steal its warmth.

I creep into bed, invite the elephants to tiptoe
across my body's pathways. When snowflakes
begin to float whitely down I close my eyes
and they melt into the soft purplish mystery
of nothing where I wish pain, all pain to vanish.

THE BLACK GLOVE

I know these rows of desks. Here's my place
which is low – long division and fear confuse me.
We're all on edge waiting for teacher to bark
the word. When it comes I lift my lid, gingerly
put my hand inside the abrasive paper bag,
clutch a boneless body with little tails.

When we're told to look inside, I pull
the woolliness out – a black glove. It magics
my mother back to life in gloves grimed
with coke. Hunched against the cold, she's lugging
the scuttle, shovelling lumps onto the fire.
It smokes angrily, then brightness licks through.

I'm tugged from flames to the coal cupboard
in the chill outside and I can't stop myself
peering into darkness which seems bottomless.
This must be what Mummy dreaded as a child
every time she had to go past the head
of the steep steps leading down to the cellar.

In her old coat she's at the front gate now
where coalmen are emptying out the sacks
they've heaved off their lorry, and she's filling
a bucket with anthracite from the black heap.
Unsmiling, she calls me to help her. Trudging
up the path, I remember gritty dust rising

from a gaping pavement grating as chunks
of coal tumbled down a chute. The air
is full of anger so I don't ask if miners work
beneath cellars but suddenly I'm in a passage
where men haloed by sickly light are hacking
for their bread. I feel their hunger for unclotted air

and try to tell them but choke on my words.
They move off and I follow but am soon lost
in tunnels, wander hopelessly until I stumble
upon a lift cage. I enter, cross my heart
as it shudders upwards. When at last I glimpse
sky-blue the black glove is still in my hand.

FIRE

Imagine this: the first time you sight
the leaping animal, its bunches of tongues
blackening the scythed grass, its potent scent
so unlike sheep or rabbit, its fiendish bite

when you stretch out to touch it – and yet
after it greys and slips away, after the sun
stops beating hard yellows on your back,
it still dances in your mind and you itch to trap it.

Imagine this: kneeling on warm grass and coaxing
the creature by rubbing a sharpened stick
against a hunk of oak until all of a sudden
it springs wildly to life, the triumph of pushing

the trapped spirit into a hollowed stone,
keeping it alive with snippets of twig and bark.
And if you feed it with pebbles when its belly's big,
wait and then shovel them into a cauldron,

the cold water will quickly eat up their heat.
Its power touches food too. Lay a plucked fowl
in its flames and the flesh soon softens,
sizzles. And in that season when light is lean,

when fog hangs blankets over the loch,
when leaves shrivel and whiteness stiffens
the barren ground you can dry wet fleeces
by hanging them above its orange lick.

And at night when you all sit round it supping,
its magic will scare the dark, drift into your songs.
Imagine this centuries away when, fumbling
with realities, you peer at red logs crumbling.

SEEING INTO THINGS

1

Leaning over the olive board
    on the table, I trace outer bark
        to inner, marvel at the precise fit of the trunk's five layers,

each scrupulous in its purpose,
    pick out sapwood, picture it piping
        water to leaves. Within lies heartwood, the tree's pillar.

Now the tree itself rises fearless
    before me but as I reach out to touch it resolves
        into a human body. Muscle lines travel to knots in the knee,

to the triangle of crotch at the thighs' apex.
    At the busy circle of stomach I come upon scars,
        lesions which will never heal, then finger the breastbone.

And as if it was possible to set breath
    in motion, I swivel the smoothed board, stumble
        upon a low-lying landscape. Its only highway is a river

which divides to slide past humps
    of treeless islands. Oh the welcome
        of wide-lipped sandy banks, easy hills in the distance.

In this place where everything is flow
    thoughts sprout like watercress, marsh marigolds.
        It's sad to have to let it go but all day I know the calm of wood.

2

Beyond the five-barred gate
        the road dwindles to a path and trees take me in.
                Their leaves speak to me in fading green, crimson, russet.

Light is playing hide and seek
        between trunks and among twig clusters.
                I envy a pair of tortoiseshells flirting in a grainy shaft of sun

as if there were no tomorrow.
        Uncertain what I'm looking for, I wander on.
                The trunks are so close now their silence presses upon me –

not Sahara silence which shouts sand
        to horizon after horizon, not the sharp blue silence
                which engulfs body and soul on a mountain summit.

This is forest silence weighted
        with the blackness between boughs
                and flickered by small wings paler than unsunned skin.

Unnerved, I kneel over a rabbit hole
        wishing I could bury fright. A hint of movement
                tells me I'm not alone, a twist of branches becomes antlers.

No, it's not imagination. Soft brown eyes
        meet mine. I enter the calm of a creature
                certain of its territory, hold my breath – the deer eyes accept me.

3

The route across shorn turf
     is tentative. Scatters of sheep bleatings above
         carry clearly as bells. From a chalk path on a fell in the distance:

a strange droning. The sound has grown
     to relentless thunder even before I come upon
         the water tumbling in torrents as if crazed. It's captured

half a leafless hawthorn tree,
     dashes its prey against boulders, hurtles it
         into the black whirlpool below. Afraid I'll be attacked,

I step back. The weight of its voice
     is unbearable, separates me from myself.
         Oh for weightlessness, a lightening of earthbound body.

I dream of floating high into sky
     like a child's transparent balloon.
         But the mighty waterfall holds me in its grip, woos

with many-runged icicles, melts them
     into fluid organ pipes. Snow feathers flutter
         across sheer rock, spindrift forms, sea wings are rising,

tiny diamonds fall in showers.
     And it takes my breath away, how white
         dissolves into black, how black resolves itself to white.

4

It's dark but a multitude of stars
     are pricking the sky with light. Lawn is unfolding
          on lawn. Not a bat flicker, not a moth flutter, the quiet is utter.

By a spinney of birch trees
     I stoop to gather silver bark peelings
          from the grass. It's then that I see the elliptical lake

and standing against the sheen:
     legs, body, one ear – the black cutout
          of a deer without antlers. It seems to be watching the moon

that's emerging as if hesitant,
     through gauzy layers into midnight's
          deep blue, to offer a tremulous path across the water.

Maybe it's because I've never seen
     anything more beautiful that the grief
          I've carried so long slips off like a heavy coat. Nothing exists

but my unclothed self,
     the moon walking across the water,
          the deer which is frostwhite now. I glimpse its single horn,

receive its wildness, its majesty,
     the mysterious healing it brings to humankind,
          At dawn the creature disappears. Unburdened, I turn for home.

The main inspiration for this sequence came from images in paintings by Robert Aldous

SPOON

A crucible for salt grains, ground pepper,
a dab of mustard, it speaks of moon –
not a harvest moon hanging heavy
as cow udders, but winter's glinting coin.

How easy to Thumbelina my body
into this bowl smooth as butter – the fit
is perfect. I lie in the curve, curled, foetal,
cosseted until a new me germinates

that's eager to explore and clinging, as if
to a rope, slides down the silver stem.
No fibres score skin, no jutting nail
stabs for blood. Feet on the floor, my dream

of miniature cracks like a walnut shell.
But it won't let me go, the container in my palm.
Though tiny it plays games with light,
has the cunning to lure the old oak beams

above my head, mutate them to a series
of molten ladders which elongate and drift down
a passage leading to a dazzle spot of lamp,
a minute triangle of window pane.

At once I abandon the brown room cluttered
with chair legs, tabletops, unyielding walls,
the claustrophobia of ceiling, enter a place
where illumination spills into unending halls.

TEAPOT

I'm warming my hands on the teapot's yellow belly
when a parakeet lands on a dead sunflower head,
snatches seeds, then flaps onto the bird-feeder

hung from our drooping clothes line. Its feathers
are woodland green, Lorca green, dream-green.
But I'm not fooled by the redberry beak, brassy eye.

No surprise that the tits scatter into the buddleia.
Yelling at this intruder into a season where beeches
have lost their copper and leaves lie in damp heaps,

is pointless – the bird ignores me, only takes off
when it's certain it can't prise out a single nut.
The coal tits are soon back but, pretty as they are,

it's no good pretending there isn't quick-nipping,
a pecking order, that given the chance they'd behave
as badly as bankers, dictators, most of us.

But why bad-mouth our species? Last week
technicians slid me into a machine conceived
by humans to explore our inner landscapes:

muscle boulders, maze of neck, the highway through
twiggeries of spine. Wrapped in insistent music
which shifted between high pitch and boom

it was as if I was encased in a huge thumping heart
or bedded in the cavern of a humpback whale
at the height of its song. And what is marvellous

is that the initiated can pinpoint sources of pain
from songs recorded in this place. Come to think of it,
thanks to our inventions, the kitchen has a music too –

a music we take for granted. Turn a tap and liquid silver
hishes. Touch a button and the washing machine
tunes up to offer purr and whirr. Flick a switch

and from the kettle comes a chant that crescendos
to a bubbling climax … I stir the tea in the pot, pour
and the tightness in my backbone loosens a little.

VISIONS OF HAWTHORN BLOSSOM

after two paintings by David Hockney

So England in May they promise wedding lace,
      stamen-freckle, our pleasant land will last for ever,
            so why not shrug off the treacheries of ice, darkness

and allow these froth fountains?
      Hedge-parsley umbels flock to a distance
            whose possibilities you couldn't exhaust, wouldn't want to.

On the verge and larger than life:
      vetch, ragged robins with straggle-pink petals.
            And you love those trees rounded as hillocks arching

over the road in emerald embrace …
      What a surprise to come upon hawthorns
            which have shed snowy clusters to pursue their own ideas.

This one's a palm – its sapphire trunk
      is tasselled with yellow poui bloom, that one's waving
            flamingo plumes. The voice of the kiskadee fills your ears

and a language more rhythmic than yours entices
      with *ball-a-fire, womb-doctor*. Magenta shadows
            creep over the road – the Soucayant waiting for nightfall?

Yet you ache as you gaze at sugarcane,
      ache as you stroll across the Savannah,
            in gardens with lawns which are scentless and too green,

ache for the smell of soft wold,
      cow-swished watermeadow, downland turf.
            So you abandon the Caribbean and step out

into a February where tired stalks
     are beginning to lift and the hawthorns
          offer reddish buds, proof that May, its mealy-semen scent

will return, that you'll breathe grass again,
     dream of kissing clusters of white blooms, pretend
          they're thornless, fool yourself blossoming will last for ever.

MAGENTA

is the dressing-gown I pounced on
      in a sale, synthetic but soft as moss furring
            damp stones in a wood. It's my keeper on a cold night.

Just to look at it is to be kindled,
      to know life needn't be dull as drizzle
            on bleached leaves or a river too muddied to welcome sky,

to know life is more than unhappiness
      poured into a phone, than pain nailing itself
            into the spine, destruction exploding in a busy street.

I search out magenta in cushions,
      cardigans, cyclamens and discover
            it has existed for aeons in the universe, is the colour

of the smallest dwarves. On our planet
      we only found a dye to produce it after
            the battle near the North Italian town that's its namesake.

Last week I heard magenta in the finale
      of Mahler's second symphony when the rumble
            of kettle drums accelerated, voices rose from brass mouths,

when the cymbals swept together,
      then separated, bloomed like giant flowers.
            Today, magenta, you are in your glory in this gallery

where so many have begged
      to be let in, the doors are now open far into
            the night – you're the earthy floor where fellowships of logs,

bold in their ochres and mustards,
        are following a coral road between blue trunks
                to the horizon. You're that rugged totem stump standing

like an old man at the junction of the road
        and a track leading to fields pink as paradise.
                I can't decide which route to take, in my head travel both.

The painting described is David Hockney's Winter Timber

OPENINGS

It's winter in Bohain – Henri Matisse is propped in bed,
his boredom with illness grey as the roofs and spatters
of snow, as the sea mists I remember from childhood.

Twenty, and the future his father's mapped for him
is boring too, like the legal documents he's expected
to spend his life penning. His mother appears at the door:

I've smuggled this up. He clicks open the child's paint box:
squares of sun-yellow, geranium, purple. Trembling,
he loads the brush, copies the watermill on the lid.

From that moment I knew this was my life.
Like an animal that plunges headlong
towards what it loves I dived in…

                               *

You can't draw, will never learn! The teacher bawling
at the raw recruit who's come to Paris to study could be
it won't do, never will red-pencilling pages of my words.

The half-open door he sketched at home, the door
in all its mystery slams shut but he copies plaster casts,
that deadly exercise he was made to do at school.

Knowing his ideas don't fit, he stumbles in self-doubt,
can only mumble when he meets Papa in Lille. Escape
is the Palais des Beaux Arts – those Goya women,

their faces burning with life, no artificial shading.
I can do this, he thinks, finds a new teacher. Years on,
that summer with an artist who'd known Van Gogh:

letting the brush sweep emerald and mustard furrows,
rushing mauve across white Brittainy skies to build
gushes of cloud. The door to colour swings open.

*

At last: the far south, feverish months in Collioure –
Collioure crouched beneath the ochres, cinnamons
and reds of foothills, a place umbrellaed by palms,

a place that stunned the rebel – its market with pyramids
of pears and tomatoes, carts spilling oranges, aubergines
like the eggs of huge birds, its whitewashed dwellings,

the sun sinking its teeth every day into bell tower, wall
and ground, killing shade. There he is: sweating, driven inside,
head swimming with watermelon-pink, periwinkle, saffron,

energy tumbling in torrents he can't stop, an energy
he's certain stems from witchcraft. *I felt only by colour,
all that mattered was construction by colour.*

Fear grips his neck as he smashes the rules of perspective,
throws out shadow, merges shapes. Night after night
panic unclothes him. Sleep flees the room, madness

looms in corners and doorways but, unstoppable, he creates
a new language for painting. Years later he said:
When I put green it is not grass, when I put blue it is not sky.

*

Hard to believe the public queued for hours outside
the Salon d'Autonne to sneer at *The Open Window*,
that critics smeared it with such contempt. Look, look

at the geraniums on its balcony. They've thrown off
plant decorum and are skipping from their capacious pots
which are so entranced with the higgle of decks and masts

out in the bay they've donned the same orange-red.
And look how easily the boats' blue hulls sit on those raspberry
and cream waves. I can't resist the open leaves of window,

the joyousness they've lured inside and I am so pulled
into this painting, so buoyed with words I lose
anchorage on the floor, float across its sea of colours.

The Impressionist who had known Van Gogh in Paris was Peter John Russell.

THE ROSAIRE CHAPEL

For months I've been compelled by the blues
and greens of these windows, the certainty
of their jubilant yellows. For months I've listened
to the nun, her singing flowering from a calm
that's white as swan and multiplying it,
for months wanted more than image on screen,
in book, wondered at the frailty that ruled
the end of his life, drove him to prise out
the essentials of colour and shape.
I've stared at elbow echoing knee in each
nu bleu, body elements shifting into abstracts
and yet woman retained – the grace of breast,
of head flowering from neck curve.
I've dipped into the time I saw the original
a decade ago when illness sapped my strength
and strange visions arose which led me down
wordpaths I'd never trodden before.
For months I've plotted a pilgrimage.

And at last you and I alight in Vence,
the May day so warm we ache to dip
our feet in the channel still running through
the elderly wash house. At last we're crossing
the narrow bridge he must have crossed
over the Luberon. I peer into the cram
of hibiscus, meadowsweet, trees. No sign of river
but the old town is crawling up the gorge,
its hug of walls crowned by the cathedral.
A dog we can't see is barking crazily
behind a gate labelled *vente de miel*
Who would dare go in, enquire for honey?

The chapel is inconspicuous and down
steep steps. Above a desk a notice

asks for silence, bans the taking of photos.
We whisper for tickets and enter. The windows
rise between stone slats like organ pipes
but the music of quiet is missing. A guide
is reading notes in monotone to bewildered faces,
mutters in many languages irritate the air,
a couple hurry in and aim cameras.
Wordless, we take refuge with an outline
of Virgin and child, then slip away,
come upon the chasubles in the museum.
Only Matisse would visualize vestments
with patterns that leap in lime, buttercup
and scarlet. Surely to don these garments
must be to know the spiritual as a release
of mind, a lightening, a skip in the heart?

A week later we re-cross the Luberon,
pass the hidden dog who's still forbidding
honey. The chapel wraps us in soundlessness.
The windows are canticles of colour,
their blue and yellow palm leaves
grow upwards in tulip pairs – and oh
the dance of cactus fronds in the panes
beyond the altar – cactus which multiplies
in the driest soil. *When I work, I believe,* his words
say themselves and I see that god is not only
creator but also the act of creating,
whatever's created without intent to destroy.
Leafy branches in the garden tremble
against the glass, the panels' violet blues
spill across the cool of marble floor
and within these white walls solidity
melts. For a little while all is luminous.

MAHLER'S NINTH

for Mary MacRae

No music in Le Pain Quotidien. Voices clatter,
crockery shrills white but the raspberries in my tartlet
are unblemished, lucent as the red in your poem.

'If it wasn't for the noise this would be perfect,'
I say, 'but we can't have everything.'
And at once I see you, my dear friend,

in a coma, hour by hour your life slipping away –
you can't have anything. I stay with you
as we join the pilgrims trailing down Exhibition Road.

In the Albert Hall everyone waits for the symphony
Mahler composed when he learnt he had an illness
doctors couldn't cure, a symphony he never heard.

Its beginning is tentative as if the instruments
are trying to find a way to talk to one another.
Phrases quiver into findings which become losings

but as the movement closes harmony's found.
Now, somewhere in the surge of strings, the poignancy
of woodwind is you, Mary, and *the brightness of red*

you want to be inside. All too soon we arrive
at the finale. The music opens out and soars
but each time it nears a climax it retreats.

How will this end – with orchestra and audience
lifting to those waterlily circles spanning
the dome? No, the instruments are quietening,

their hushed voices hover, fall away.
There isn't anything now but the five thousand
held together in a silence larger than sound.

BEETHOVEN'S NINTH

Nothing is sweeter to my ears than the voice
of someone I love, soothing words from a stranger,
voices of doves in summer trees, the joy
which emerges in the finale of Beethoven's Ninth.

Nothing is more frustrating than failing to follow
a fast or subdued talker, than hearing conversation
as a loud blur in a room of faces but this is minor.
What does a composer suffer if sound diminishes

to nothing and he can only unfold in his head
the music he's created? Imagine Beethoven
at that first performance of his final symphony,
a gesticulating figure standing beside the conductor,

rising, shrinking, stretching forward as if he wanted
to be all the instruments, every singer in the choir,
and still immersed when the work reached its end,
unaware of the applause until the contralto

turned him round to see the audience on their feet,
hands clapping, hats being thrown up into the air,
mouths uttering what could only be 'bravo'.

LOST

after Chagall: Adam et Eve chassés du Paradis

There is no music now in paradise.
The garden's ripped by cries of consternation,
a blinding white circle of face belongs

to a figure whose body is flower-blur
and stems twinned with leaves, a figure
inseparable from this place, its din.

There is no music now in paradise.
Tranquillity is a shrivelled fruit, trees
wrenched from roots are hurtled to the sky,

birds plummet to ocean, stampeding hooves
smash grasses. The tempter's vanished,
panic-bitten humans are in flight.

There is no music now in paradise.
The word *sin* hisses in ears, guilt
lays its eggs, hearts work like clappers,

selves are in tatters. Though daisies
will rise again, moments gleam with sound
there is no music now in paradise.

THE FOOTHILLS OF THE WHITE MOUNTAINS

What garden could possibly bloom
on this desiccated earth? Not lupined borders,
not lemon-throated lilies, hollyhocks, roses.

A trunk blackened by fire is standing sentry
at the gate and a gust rips into our clothes
but as we clamber past flaccid stalks
we are suddenly surrounded by flocks of trees,

gasp at ripe papayas, species of palm and guava
I didn't know existed. Fig leaves finger us,
a banana plant offers a yellow-penis flower

but I sidle past it to a passion of red blossoms –
their fruit will be Song of Solomon's pomegranates.
Oh think of the ruby flesh within the split globes,
those seeds Persephone couldn't resist!

Down, slowly down the track slippery as bone
to touch cliffs with many lips trickled by water
and sit sipping from bottles in an arbour
among purple petals weightless as butterflies,

to gape at a strangely emerald pool far below,
at hills humped high into the sky, the shock
of buzzard wings – their utter stillness.

And though I've not yet come upon the aromatics,
sniffed dittany, pennyroyal, Ophelia's rue,
not yet bowed to the myrtle Venus loved, descended
to the old cart by the pool, found the orange groves,

though I've not begun to unravel the mystery
of the charred trunks marking out the route:
four brothers' memorial to a terrible fire

which burnt many thousands of olive trees,
some centuries old, I already know this eden,
fecund as the imagination, is the original garden –
the garden we lose however often we come upon it.

The Botanical Centre, Crete

GOLD

I'm transfixed by a pair of bees, not bees
searching for pollen, gold bees in the museum
at Heraklion, each with a leaflike wing and circle of eye

balancing the other. The beautiful segments
of their abdomens curve until they join
in copulation. The two nurse a drop of honey.

When I try to imagine the refined lady who lived
in painted rooms being robed, then adorned
with the necklace on which this jewel hung,

I see beyond this gold to the potency of another –
bowlfuls of small fruits with glistening black
and green skins, fruit which pleased the mouth

or was pressed into lucent liquid, poured into
amphorae taller than men and stored in the depths
of Minoan palaces, a gold which cooked food

and fed lamps, that cleansed sweating bodies
and cured the sick, a gold so valuable that scribes
recorded it on tablets: the oil as a pair of rivering lines,

the crucial tree with its arms stretched out,
the plump fruits dominant on branches. No wonder
that Athena's gift to the Greeks of olive trees

was prized above Poseidon's war horses.
And I'm not surprised when the girl calls me
into her shop brimming with long-necked bottles

and soaps in wicker nests, softens my hands
with olive cream, when every restaurant owner
greets us with gold: a gleaming smile, a dish of olives.

ORANGES

They outnumber the visitors clambering
from coaches, the huge crowds of flowers peering
from gardens. We point at them nested in trees,
hammocked in net bags hanging from door knobs,
bedded cheek to cheek in baskets outside gates.
El Greco, who the inhabitants insist was born
in this village, is dimmed by their multitudes.
Sevesdiana nods as she leads us into a café.
How eagerly a pair of weathered sisters
open their arms to hug her. How warmly
they greet us, her charges. How quickly
pressed orange juice, little breads and Nescafé
are laid on a round table. The brown counter,
fading walls and metallic zigzags on the freezer
whisper the musty past but the talk glitters.
Before we leave we're each given an orange
English supermarkets would boo and bin,
a giant orange with bumps, dents, niggles
and an offbeat attempt at rotundity,
a fruit quite unabashed by its rusticity.

In the blue morning light that's swum
into our room overlooking Chania harbour
you and I each peel one – a mother-of-oranges.
I expect the pith to be thick, the heart of the matter
small and maybe tart, but the skin is thin,
pliable, the segments vast. Sprawled on the bed,
I cram one into my mouth. Its juice spurts
over the sheet and the tangy sweetness tastes
of Fodele's trees creeping from the streets
to clothe steep slopes, of laces white as frost
and home-woven rugs hung from strings
to attract tourists. It tastes of a solid back

bending to scrub a carpet splayed on the road,
of the women holding out the sugared breads
that were blessed in church for a friend's birthday.
It tastes – it tastes of those rare moments
when a silence suspends the ordinary
and the unattainable seems within reach.

APTERA

Not only marvelling at the reds of pimpernel and poppy,
    the sprinklings of canary-yellow daisies in fretworks of stalk,
        the everywhere oleanders and the olive trees, their thin leaves
            freckled with snowy bobbles, growing ramshackle on the steep slope –

not only rubbing up against unlabelled history as we climb
    steps going nowhere from the stump of a massive stone wall,
        sight lopped but still-standing columns, flutings on tumbled lintels
            and one of the once-city's roads that's now too mangled to walk on –

not only watching a posse of sheep panic on this peak
    above Souda Bay, then revelling in the benevolent orange earth,
        the dark purple of not-to-be-meddled-with mountains and the sky's
            sagging belly as rain suddenly begins to sweeten the parched ground.

But also savouring the good humour, in idiomatic English,
    of the woman who runs the café where we sit under a rush roof
        eating baked tomatoes, their plumped cheeks full of saffron rice,
            with un-supermarket meat cooked in terracotta to utter tenderness –

also her banter with three young German cyclists
    who have just discarded bikes and gear for a lunch break
        in their tough tour of Crete's hills, and are tucking into salads
            with feta cheese that runs easily as the woman's generosity –

and also this *now*, the taste and texture of it on an island
    I've waited all my life to visit, the cock crowing in a garden as if
        calling from my faraway childhood, the patch where potato plants
            compete with cactuses, this *now* of drinking in the world's goodness.

GARDEN

At last the rain has ceased so open
the back door and go down the steps,
breathe in the herbiness of oregano,

wander among the flocks of marguerites,
pat the old pear tree, watch the butterflies:
their flitterings, momentary couplings, alightings,

the brief unfoldings of wings stamped
with crimson dusk. Go, go to the boughs
weighted with Worcesters, their cheeks red

as those of the wicked queen's apple. Forgive
the buddleia for toppling over the courgettes –
you love its purple desire to grow.

The warmth loosening the ache trapped
in your bones urges that ageing
and in the end withering are inevitable.

A rustle, and Eliot's *quick said the bird*
utters itself in your head. You go back
but it's not to the rose garden,

not to the *drained pool*, not to the pool
filled with water out of sunlight.
Look, you're in that first garden, the eden

you took for granted. Two of you
are hurrying pails of water down steps
past the rose of sharon bushes

whose long-stamened petals are too dull
for your imagination. Much better is the earth
you muddy by the sandpit, trowel for gold,

till losing patience with stones which refuse
to budge, you monkey up the climbing frame
and in a trice reinvent it as a flying carpet …

Oh childhood where the present
is unfenced, time a flat, shiny face
with meanings you've not yet learnt to read,

and the immense far ahead can be moulded
into any shape you choose! Gone,
gone, the chime that insisted every hour

but what does it matter? You know too well
how the years have shrunk your future,
that the past is an ever-expanding suitcase.

Look, the wooden climbing frame
has slid into the metal one that's beyond
the lilac and your own child's yelling:

'We must kill this forest fire!' as he
and his friend haul up bucket after bucket
to douse branches of irrepressible elder.

You blink – the frame is rusted, straggled
with honeysuckle, the boys have long
grown into men. *Now* pushes you

to your feet, to the bees still milking
flowering raspberries. You free a frog
from the net, watch it hop back to its life.

CLOUD

Dusk: behind the blurring railway bridge
a row of December roofs is emerging
and long-disused chimneys are stamped

on luminous apricot like repeating
paper cut-outs a child has carefully pasted
into her scrap book. Above tree laceries

a cloud soft as the line of roofs swells into
a scalloped sea animal and glides across
the panes in the bay window. The day's demands

slip from my shoulders as the creature humps
and begins to caterpillar into low islands.
The movement is so slow, so effortless

in what is now an ocean of faintest blue
it seems to be part of the stillness. I wish
I could think that what I'm looking at is heaven;

to people in the seventh century *heofan* and sky
were a single word. I can't believe
the divine exists in a fixed place overhead –

isn't god the energy driving the universe,
the dimensions of its mathematics visible
in patterns on this planet, the union of sperm

and egg, our compassionate connections
with one another, small selves drifting
into the damson wings of darkening clouds?

NOT YET

Five-thirty, mid-March, and already
day has begun. Frost lies in strips
across the park, across our lawn.
Soon the sun will have licked it up,
skimmed the air of cold. I want
to kiss the fistfuls of buds
the half-dead pear tree is offering,
and the winter-thin honeysuckle clinging
to the once-climbing frame.
Above the iron spider of Alexandra Palace
three-quarters of the moon is jutting
from a slit in a blue sky
clear as a bell. A tube train,
eyes glinting, is weaving itself
between trees and roofs. I don't want it
to vanish underground – not yet.

If only I could trap this moment
in cupped hands before it's flown,
stave off the knock on the door, the chill
rushing up my nightdressed body,
if only I could stave off the paper thudding
on the mat, the unfolding in the kitchen
of the man cradling his wounded brother,
the uncontainable grief – if only
I could pretend time is a clock
whose arrow hands I could pull off,
and stay here dreaming myself
into the copse in the park, floating
among all the wood anemones
about to open white wings.

BEYOND

Running

He's dipping a red umbrella
into grass skinny as himself,
grass that's already flopping, pale
as his face, his raincoat, your thoughts.

The fumble of age in his step –
or is he blind? No, he's away
in his grey gabardine, darting,
dotting. Not a shadow of doubt –

he's been let loose from lifeless rooms,
is a boy running and roughing
in fields he's not smelt for decades.
Or is it you who's running out

to breathe in cow-warmth, you haring
from a devil about to hurl
a stone? Quick! to the brook, gym shoes
sinking into mud and marsh gold …

The small zigzags come to a stop
and he turns. You have a vision
not of a foolish Lear but one
whose face is lit up with sheer joy.

And all that day you see nothing
but white grass that's wilting, wild hair,
a scarlet umbrella pointing.
All day you're smote by happiness.

Fog

This place is detached from everywhere else.
You watch the way the hide-and-seek sun
drops spots of gold on the icy lake,

stare at rectangles warning of danger.
Geese and seagulls are in huddles as if fearing
doomsday. Don't stop to feed them –

the whiteness is growing from moment
to moment, eating deep into your body.
The doubling of trunks and twiggeries

makes you catch your breath but you know
there's as much duplicity here as in the everyday.
Enter the beckoning pale and dark of this world

and it will stop your heart. You can't fly
so don't flutter fingers or raise your arms,
keep moving. A playground's slide looms,

disappears half way down. The sun is now
as white as the whitest moon. Soon you will lose
both partner and path. There will be nothing.

Posting

When you stuff letters into its mouth
you wonder why it's labelled Thursday –
today's Monday. Silence is a cloud

overhead and you know in your heart
this mail will never be collected,
that in months envelope will moulder

into beige envelope. Peer inside
the rectangular shout and you'll glimpse
a glinting dog that's waiting to snatch

gobbets of happiness and remnants
of self-respect. The moment it's chewed
the present it will paw the future,

this mangy cousin of the black two-
headed hound that's on permanent guard
at death's gate. Forget the red overcoat –

it may be gaudy as hips and haws
or Father Christmas but the colour
is bonfire. Listen, sticks are cackling,

orange demons stoking up. Don't song
and dance with the flames, move off before
you're posted to the everlasting.

Night

A silence edgy with minute sounds –
from your imagination perhaps,
and on the landing floor a long pane
so luminous it is a presence.

Wanting to know its source, you cut off
street lights by closing a bedroom door
but the shape persists. You place yourself
by the landing window, outstretch arms –

the oblong's not deterred – you can feel
its determination. Downstairs
visitants are everywhere: a dull
green eye fixes you from the freezer,

a red one from the phone, stars cluster
round the computer. Drawn back upstairs
you're still foxed – how did the presence
contrive to travel through solid walls?

You open a window, crane upwards
and it's there – just touching the roof's rim,
more subtle than the sun, bright as hope.
The joy of moon is inside your house.

CAFFÈ NERO

You watch juice whirled with ice to froth
and crowned with a transparent dome,
a pleasure dome which hypnotizes light,
invites fingers to stroke, then in the easy
air-conditioned cool, you suck mango liquid
through a straw black as espresso coffee,
crumple up thoughts as if they were tissues,
taste paradise. Through glass you see not darkly
but clearly, the Bishop of Winchester's palace,
a shell hemmed in by a warehouse
and sadly cross-hatched by scaffolding
but the mediaeval tracery in its rose window
is still intact. You remember that just upriver
the new Globe promises an hour or so
of Shakespeare experience and expect Cleopatra
in her burnished barge, purple sails flying.
But she's not on the water, she's by a doorway
on her mobile phone. With her lime trouser suit
and olive skin she stands above the hosts
of Saturday people on the waterfront.
Like you they've left at home the realities
they find hard to bear. Decked out
in over-short shorts, tangerine saris,
t-shirts strained over lumpy stomachs,
they're ice-cream lickers with wires fixed
in their ears, smilers with prams and dogs –
look at that dog, teeth deep into its lead,
swung by its owner a metre off the ground.
And all this cram and jostle of London
is incongruous as your self – as all selves.
And though you could weep at your own,
at the world's bagfuls of unresolvables,
sitting with your shining dome of juice
in the café's cool on this last of June,
you are suddenly jubilant to be alive.

SNACK BAR

after Edward Burra

Is it the loud lights that pull you in or the glimpse
of a woman with scarlet lips, her elbows nonchalant
on the long white counter, or the bodies

of cured meats hanging in a row above
glistening trays of beetroot, chopped tomato
and pickled cucumber? Jazz rhythms begin in your head:

syncopations on the piano, hurtlings from a huge
silver mouth – this is life as you've never known it.
But even as you step inside you can see

there's too much knife and fork and the slices
he's cutting with such concentration from the salami
are a worry; they're too pink and creeping

off the board surreptitiously as if planning
an undercover attack as soon as he looks away.
As for her, she's barely aware of the sandwich

she's pushing between her reddened lips
and for all its lavish fur collar and cuffs you can tell
her coat offers her no refuge from the cold.

She can't even squeeze a drop of milky warmth
from the imitation pearls adorning her ears.
Oddly, there's not a trace of quiet though no one

is saying a word – not her, she's miles away;
not the obsessed salami hacker, not the old guy,
too thin for his mac, sitting on a stool at the back.

The listlessness is a grey mutter, the raw bulbs
shout at your eyes, high-pitched argument
is pushing in from the street. A saxophone

lifts its voice and its melancholy wanders
into this anycity place. It's so full of her loneliness
you could cry. You want to leave but her eyes

fix you as if you've always known her, as if
you were her – she can't be shaken off. Admit it,
deep down she's always dwelt inside you.

ON THE TRAIN

Sometimes when the computer's in sulk,
when you've failed to appease your partner,
mother, child or cat, when you've hurried
down roads hoping to escape the conundrum
of yourself or limped from the dentist's to daylight
with all the stuffing knocked from body and mind
even though pain is no longer boring into your teeth,
all you can do is climb chilling flights of steps,
clamber on board and thank god or your lucky stars
that no one's bellowing the obvious into a mobile.
All you can do is gaze at the backsides of houses,
their clumsy sheds and drooping lines of washing,
at hoardings, factories, and outbursts of October leaves,
at glints from sudden streams, interludes of grass.
All you can do is accept the sumptuous dark of chocolate
melting in your mouth, gaze at the magenta lipstick
filling a double-spread in the magazine you picked up
at Whistlestop, imagine buying it though you never
colour your face, then feel inferior as you read
about the woman who rules the National Trust.
All you can do is smack shut the complacent pages
and look at the everyday girl who's sitting opposite.
Her pinkish high-heeled shoes are fragile as slippers,
her face is creased with fatigue. You doubt she could rule
a pocket-sized kitchen or a stack of pots in a shed
but you can't take your eyes off her handbag,
its amber clip, the silvergold lustre of its fabric,
the zips to its many enticing compartments.

IN THE BAG

My, that's some handsome bag you've got!
The voice, soft and grainy as Muscovado sugar,
makes me smile. I peer at its British Museum's
plastic hieroglyphics. The bus lurches.

I'm wondering why I've never examined
the delicate birds and bowls and snakes,
each a meaning I can't decipher
                                 when I discover
a bomb is stowed underneath my folders.

Terrified I'm a danger, might be branded *terrorist*,
I scramble off, risk traffic at an intersection,
hurry through foggy streets in a fever to rid myself
of the package, at last come upon my house.

Indoors, such relief as I sniff familiarity
and fill the kettle – but look, I'm still holding
the dangerous bag.
                      I rush it down the garden
as far as the compost heap and its smell of rot,

reach inside, pull out a baby and two potatoes.
Once I've bedded the child on yellowed
cabbage leaves I gaze at its flawless body,
at its face which is untroubled as a china doll's.

Is the bomb the smaller or the bigger potato?
I hurl them both over the fence into the park,
hold my breath.
                    They land among the meanest flowers
and I tremble, not knowing what I've planted.

JOURNEYS

It's when I lose patience
with the self-satisfied expressions
of girls in next summer's bikinis –
the way they're rubbing sleek shoulders
with the rising figures of the jobless –
and slap the paper shut that I realize
I've no idea if we've been facing
the same black panes of tunnel
for minutes or hours.
I listen now to the mumble
that keeps weaving itself
into the clogged silence. Pointless.
I can't even detect from the tone
if the outlook is hope or doom.

Mute resignation has fallen
like dust over the compartment
where I'm wedged between an oldish
and podgy Chinese man,
whose elbow obtrudes into my space,
and a woman whose face is chalked
with fatigue. Her English is broken
but I gather the tannoyed messages
mean nothing to her either.
And just as it hits me that nobody
has extracted any information
the Chinese man swivels
to face me and lets out a torrent
of indecipherable distress.
I nod, hoping I'm expressing sympathy.

Trying to blot out that words have failed us,
that we are each quite alone
in a pocket of self, I watch
a woman bulging out of her trousers
bite into a bumper bar of chocolate
with a ferocity which is daunting.
I've nothing to eat
except a squashed cough lozenge.
Suppose the train doesn't move
today, tomorrow, ever,
how long before the oxygen
in this impure air is used up?

I take a deep breath and immediately
panic I'm going to suffocate
so I rummage in my bag for my book.
A mountain soars on the cover,
its precipices, snow-laden shoulders,
sharp faces, carry a raven sky.
At once I'm raw seventeen,
climbing from flowered meadows
to high above the treeline,
I'm in a cot hewn from rock, too close
to the smell and bodies of others
to slip into sleep,
I'm wrapped in a blanket
stumbling out to the gush of icy air,
gaping from my smallness
at the circle of peaks around me
as the sun dazzles their darkness
with blazing orange,
commands summit after summit
to sing in saffron and pink…

One glance inside my book
and a longing to be in mountain immensity
scrambling upwards to blue air,
overwhelms me.
Is that why the quest of a traveller
who's risking almost impossible passes
in the world's highest country
is so compelling,
why I'm searching through his eyes
for signs of the snow leopard
to satisfy an indefinable need
and why I'm learning to accept
nothing will be found on this expedition
but tracks and bones from the kills
of that smoky or yellowish cat whose coat,
printed with streaks and spots of black,
is beautiful beyond words?

A jerk. The Himalayas dissolve –
the train is moving but fitfully
as a reluctant mule. It comes
to a halt at Wood Green
which at street level boasts
no wood and little green.
Scowling and muttering to himself,
the Chinese man scurries away.
Minutes pass but the mule won't shift.
Others exit crossly but at last
it budges, at last emerges
to roofs and trees doused in light.
I climb a flight of steps
into the joyous March afternoon,
and in three minutes I'm in the park
where the air smells of grass,
where the gulls, which were lined up

in cohorts on the playing fields
this morning as if awaiting orders,
are now strolling in desultory fashion
and nodding, pecking, wing-flapping.
Why, I want to ask them –
though there's no language
we can share and they'd screech
at my absurdity if they could –
why, I long to ask, do they abandon
ocean and beach to journey inland,
install themselves in my suburban park?

The Snow Leopard by Peter Mattheissen

FINDING SILENCE

Dictionaries define the word in negative terms:
muteness, reticence, taciturnity, noiselessness.
The second volume of The Shorter Oxford English
does include *quiet* in its weighty considerations

but fails to recognize that at the heart of it
is presence, not absence. I think I already knew
when I was a child running through the wildness
of the moors that silence was a dimension of sound

for there it was fed by curlew cries, by the wind
rushing through untidy cotton-grass and clumps
of marsh marigold, by sheep baaing and great
grey ships honking far below on the Firth of Clyde.

Silence isn't a plant to be cultivated in a solitary house
perched on a hill, not the cave single-minded seekers
hunt out so that they can contemplate meanings
away from the hurly-burly of the over-peopled world

with its cash machines and quarrels, ceaseless phones,
splashes of laughter. Silence is that small place
we come upon, the patch we clear to be with our selves
in shop, train, lane, doctor's waiting room – anywhere.

THE MINOTAUR

It's still alive in my head – how could it not be? – that morning
when I first grasped what I was, that morning when I woke
in the wintry sniff of my bed's old olive leaves and grasses,

my head full of knots, my heart heavy as a grinding stone.
Grumbling at the wind for whipping my skin, chilling my bones,
I scrambled from the cave I'd made my home down to the valley.

You see I was lonely, so lonely by myself – that's why I stopped
to watch the cattle chewing cud and crept close enough to gulp
the milky smell of them. The air was strung tight as a lyre's strings

and excitement shot through me when a bull mounted a cow.
I remembered the wrinkled thing between my legs, how it had a will
of its own, how just before sleep it swelled faster than a ripening fruit

and spilled its juice if I pictured a woman's haunches or her breasts.
It fattened then and, wishing I had a mate, I gaped at calves sucking
from udders. The animals' breath was suddenly mine and I found

I was lowing urgently and hurrying towards them. They all looked up,
the air prickled with rage and the bull snorted, lowered its horns,
charged. I saved myself by jumping over a wide stream

but it struck me like a smack on the muzzle – the truth I'd not faced:
I was neither man nor beast, I was a nothing creature out of place
in the world. As if food was stuck in my gullet I began to choke.

When my breath quietened I stared into the stream and there
in the clear waters was a hideous bull's head. Its jaws were open,
contorted as if in pain. Then I saw it had the body of a man,

a muddy thing that was clad in the remains of a robe . A bellow
filled my ears – it was mine! Shivering, I gawped at myself, a self
I'd not seen before. The one I had inside me was only an idea

fuzzy as a dream. Of course I knew my horns singled me out.
While they were growing my mother would stroke them, tell me
they were a splendid gift from the gods. Her praise made me think

my head was like a crown – a thing of glory. But now, oh listen
if you will, now I saw what a freak I was and I threw myself down
on a rock, my mind full of bite, roared at Pasiphae, my dear mother

who was far away, lost for ever, how wicked she'd been to hide
the truth from me. At last when I'd bellowed myself hoarse,
my mind filled up with my childhood, prancing on her carpets,

clambering into her bed, nuzzling into her sleepy skin. I began to see
she'd meant to shield me from people's hatred, that because of her
I hadn't cared when the other children taunted and played tricks.

All that mattered was her and being outside in the garden,
pulling up handfuls of grass, rubbing the green smell into my skin
and chewing the stalks for sap. I loved being in Pasiphae's rooms

but I felt cooped indoors, itched to get out. Often I begged her
to let me go beyond the palace walls. Now I knew why she'd refused,
told me violently it was too dangerous. Tears rolled down my face

as I remembered how I would rush outside after it rained, roll over
and over in the grass until I was soaked, put my ear to the ground,
listen to a nameless pounding that called and called me.

Soon I was reliving, and with new eyes, the day everything changed.
I was almost fully grown, often argued and disobeyed but I tell you
I was more ignorant than a young boy, a bullock in a herd.

King Minos, who I'd rarely seen and only at a distance, strode
into my mother's rooms. I hated the het-up smell of him, the lines
of cruelty on his coarse face so I kept out of sight behind a curtain.

The air grew heavy, stank with threat and my neck stiffened
as I sensed something terrible was going to happen. Pulling off
his purple robe, he grabbed Pasiphae's chin and growled:

'I want you now.' Her face was crumpling to cry but he smacked it
and ripped her tunic. Furious, I threw myself on him to save her
from his attack. Pinning his elbows to his sides, I sank my teeth

into his spine and when I saw I'd made two rows of bite marks
which were sprouting crimson blood I was pleased and licked
my lips. But he swung round, felled me to the ground with his fists,

yelled: 'Flesh eater.' Then he kicked me hard, so hard the walls
began to spin but I wasn't afraid. Fool that I was I tried to butt him
with my horns, only shrank back when I saw the look of horror

on my mother's face. In seconds soldiers ran in. Minos snatched
a spear from one and ran it down my face. Then I was dragged
a long way through courtyards I'd never visited, glimpsed

statues of gods and winged creatures and gold hangings in rooms.
When we reached a yard that smelt of dung I was thrust into a cage.
I hurled myself against the door but it was barred and I was alone

with an animal stench I didn't recognise. My thoughts swarmed
like bees and in a frenzy to rescue my mother from that brutal man
I thrust my whole weight against the walls but nothing buckled,

nothing broke. My rage burned on but by the time daylight died
my mind was packed with fears I'd never known. You can imagine
how I paced my prison, sweating, swatting at insects. At last I lay down

and looked up at a tiny star through a hole in the roof, pretended
it was Pasiphae's bright face and fell asleep. When I woke I saw
a dead goat stretched out by the door and scratched my head,

puzzled that this one was lying in its blood. Then I prickled –
goats were kept for milk and I was afraid the creature was a sign
I'd be murdered too. I saw a jar of water standing beside it, then a bag

hanging from one of the bars across the window gap in the wall
and I trembled for I knew before I found the apricots and grapes
they were a present from my mother. Under the fruit was a letter:

'Dear son, we cannot meet again but I will always be in your heart.
Trust me, be brave. A friend of mine, who has much knowledge,
is working out a plan to save you. Destroy these words at once

and eat all the food I send – you must hold onto your strength.'
I forced myself to obey and tried not to lose hope but many weeks
passed and it petered out as a brook does that's starved of rain.

I hated the filth in the cage and the dead goat was decaying,
covered with flies and fleas. It stank so I scraped and scraped
at the ground until at last I managed to bury it in the dust and dirt.

Next morning a ram lay by the jar of daily water and in my head
I heard the king's voice again roaring: 'flesh eater'. Then I knew
this man, more evil-minded than any beast, had spread the news

that I guzzled on animals and decided to make this a reason
to keep me in prison for ever. I leapt up as if I'd been stung
and, snorting, smashed my horns against a wall again and again.

You must see that I, who had always pined for grass and sky,
would sink into madness if I this was to be my life? When the sun fell
on my cage and dug its claws into my back, I bellowed in desperation.

But suddenly she was standing in front of me, my mother bright
as a jewel, her arms full of grasses and lilies from her garden.
I pressed them against my face, sniffed the freshness and sobbed

as her gentleness enfolded me like a sheet. She hushed me
with firm words as she did when I was little and ran wild. 'Be patient,
Minotaur, in one week you will leave this place. My friend, Daedalus

was ordered by Minos to use his skills to construct a great labyrinth
to house you. Secretly, he's built a tunnel from it into a gorge.
Now, listen carefully. When you're taken to the maze you must stop

at each turning and find the circle scratched on the wall. These signs
will guide you to a ravine which will lead you to a distant valley.
Then you will live in freedom, roam the land, find wild goats to milk

and fruit to pick. You must leave no sign of yourself, let no one see you.'
Excited, I gabbled questions, tried to hug her but she'd disappeared.
How I wrestled with hope and fear all week but on the seventh morning

as light cracked, men invaded my cell, put me in chains and prodded me
down steps until we were far underground. Here they unbound me
and cursing, kicked me into the maze. There were more turnings

than a pomegranate has seeds but at each I managed to discover
the promised sign and at last I was walking between giant blocks
of rock, saw sky blue as cornflowers above me. The path widened

and I came to a river where I knelt and gulped mouthfuls of water.
The sun was reddening by the time a great grassiness opened out.
I flung myself down on the ground and happiness rushed through me

like the loud white tumble of a waterfall – do you know how it feels
to be shut in prison and then set free? That night and next day
I kept murmuring thanks to my mother and her friend for saving me.

All summer I revelled in rolling on red earth, climbed rugged mountains, watched eagles soaring, crept silent as a vole into thickets, picked almonds in furry coats, purple pouches of figs, olives black as night.

I rounded up goats, learnt to milk them – patted their firm bodies, sniffed them on my hands. I stroked the skin of the sea which I'd never been close to before, loved its shiver, its cool waters licking my skin.

But when winter pelted rain and bullied me with winds, the loss of my mother, a longing for people was more painful than belly ache. Loneliness filled my eyes and ears, seeped into my sleep at night.

As I lay on that cold rock looking back at my life I saw again servants eyeing me with disgust, smelt the sneering men who'd shoved me into the maze and despair crushed me again with its terrible teeth.

It was night now, moonless night and I begged death to take me, wished that I'd never been born. As if in answer wings flapped and a yellow-eyed owl alighted on a branch above my head,

wavered into Pasiphae, her face a moon – oh more than moon. There stood the only person who felt love for me yet I howled at her: 'How cruel you were, how cruel not to tell me what I was.'

She clasped my shoulders but her face was stern: 'Dear Minotaur, listen to me, I knew you'd only survive if I fed you love, cradled you in safety and made you happy enough to believe your worth.

But I told you no lies – I am certain you are a sign from the gods that human and animal kind are closely related. You're as strong now as Atlas who took the mighty weight of the world on his shoulders.

Tonight you must trample on despair. Tomorrow you must return to the maze – you are going to shed your solitary life just as a snake sheds its skin.' I began to argue but wings flapped, she was gone.

*

I must have slept for at dawn I was lying on the rock. I remembered
I'd dreamt of moons and Pasiphae, her powerful words. My head
grumbled but I obeyed her commands. The moment I stepped inside

the web of passages I caught a whiff of humans and crouched –
you'd have done so too. Then I smelt and saw a rotting animal. Fear
thumping my whole body, I wondered if the vision was a trick.

I crept backwards but bumped into someone, snorted in terror.
It was a girl whose face was too thin and her eyes were full
of shock. My grotesque head in the water flashed into my mind

and I heard myself whisper: 'I won't hurt you.' 'Oh,' she whispered
and half-smiled as if she trusted me. Her friendliness brought a lump
to my throat and I croaked: 'Follow me, I'll lead you to a place of safety.'

She nodded. When we'd trudged to the end of the gorge, I watched
while she gulped slicks of water from the river as I'd done the day
I escaped. I gave her an apple I'd picked yesterday. She ate it hungrily.

When she'd finished I asked her who she was and in a voice
sweet as bird music she said: 'My name's Arminta and I was sent
with twelve others from Greece as tribute to your king and a feast

for the monster in the maze.' The words crashed on me like boulders –
only her face, unfrightened, stopped me from stamping and roaring
but I couldn't help choking out: 'I've never eaten flesh human or animal,

I wouldn't even kill a slithering worm. Minos must have made up this lie,
he hates me, I'm so different.' 'I am too,' she sighed. Then her face
turned milk-white and she swayed. Ashamed I'd been so clumsy –

you see it was obvious she was weak with hunger – I said: 'Come
with me, I'll give you food and shelter.' By the time I'd helped her
up the steep, stony hill to my cave, night was devouring the scarlet sun.

In the dusk we sat and ate hunks of cheese and nuts, drank milk,
then slept. Light, nosing at the entrance, pulled me to my feet
next morning. I looked at my sleeping friend, longed to lick her cheeks

but knew this would be wrong so I went outside and as I milked
the goats, Pasiphae's words about my loneliness coming to an end,
flowed into my mind. The sun was high, an eye staring down at the world,

when Arminta came out, drank thirstily and told her story: 'My father –
he's the king's brother – groomed his daughters to be princesses, play
the lyre, sew and sit on couches in silk robes looking seductive.

All this bored me – perhaps that's why I was bad at embroidery.
What I wanted was to go outside and explore, learn which plants
were food, which medicines. In any case I'm no beauty to wear silks.'

'Oh but you are,' I burst out, 'with your olive eyes, soft hair
and your smile – you're lovely as an iris.' 'You've not seen my sisters
and look I've been branded by the gods.' She pulled off a sandal.

There was webbing between her toes and by the smallest a claw.
'My parents believe these deformities are an evil portent –
they made use of the tribute to be rid of me.' I stroked her foot

and oh love bounded through me! Arminta murmured:
'The night before we sailed I dreamt of a tall shadowy figure
with shapely white horns and anemones on his head. He promised

he wouldn't hurt me and I awoke full of hope.' We fell silent then
but my heart was full of singing and the sniff of her was so fragrant
in the air. Suddenly she pointed: 'Look, a swallowtail sucking pollen.'

I was gazing at the butterfly's beautiful black latticed wings,
when she exclaimed: 'You're lucky to live here on a hill throbbing
with insects and such clumps of flowers.' 'I will be,' I blurted,

'if you stay with me.' Arminta smiled, touched my arm – oh the leap
inside me. That night I kissed her toes, her haunches, nuzzled
her breasts. Our mouths became little animals searching for each other

and excitement pounded like many hooves through my blood
until in a heat which rose like unstoppable flames and in a joy
I tell you I had no idea existed, the two of us were sealed together.

That was the beginning of our shared happiness. In summer
we scrambled to mountain tops, gazed at buzzards, at the world lying
below us and Arminta taught me all she knew about plants.

When winter chilled our bodies we sat by the crackling fire while it fed
our faces and bellies with warmth, told stories from our lives. Seasons
passed. Then one night I saw towering flames in the valley below.

They were so fierce the burn of them stung my nostrils. I asked
my wife, 'What can they mean?' Seeing how troubled I was she put
an arm round me, said: 'Tomorrow, dear heart, I'll go and find out.'

Soothed, I fell asleep but dreamt I was trapped in the maze, struggling
to find circles. Then I saw a scrawny old bull limping along a passage.
At once a figure sprang from nowhere, drew a sword and drove it deep

into the helpless animal. I tottered as though he'd struck me too.
When it fell to its death I watched, appalled, as he jabbed
the carcass again and again roaring: 'I've killed the Minotaur!'

In spite of the fear blocking my throat, something compelled me
to follow the sniff of this monstrous and arrogant man and I soon saw
he was retracing a route he'd marked out by unwinding a ball of string.

Suddenly I found myself in dazzling sunlight among a huge crowd
in a palace courtyard but no one noticed me. All eyes were fixed
on the warrior who was now decked in garlands and seated on a dais

next to Minos. The king proclaimed: 'Theseus, hero, I thank you
for ridding us of the terrible Minotaur who glutted himself on youths
and maidens. Your name will resound for ever throughout the world'.

He pointed at a girl – I saw she was my slyest sister – and said grandly:
'My daughter is yours, let there be feasting and dancing round fires
all night.' I tried to yell: 'That man's a liar!' but a cloud descended

and I was alone in a dark place until I saw a pale shadow that turned
into Pasiphae. 'Theseus is a coward, I've been wrongly accused,'
I burst out. She put a hand on my muzzle: 'My child, I know all this

but I'm afraid it's the way of the world. Many are heaped with prizes
they don't deserve, the brave and the brilliant are often unrewarded.
Others, like you, are turned into victims. But you have a golden gift –

happiness, rejoice in it.' She kissed me. The next thing I knew
it was morning and Arminta was holding out a bowl of milk.
When I related my dream she took both my hands and said:

'Your mother is wise and what matters is that you know the truth
in your heart, trust those who love you.' Oh she was so right,
my dear one. Our quiet life continued – I forgot there was any other.

Then one warm day we were by the sea gathering conical shells
whose whorls were marked with violet squares and fine bands
of silver-pink as if a sensitive god had painted each with a feather-tip.

'Once these were houses for minute creatures,' Arminta murmured.
She added as if her words were nothing special, 'It's time I told you
our child is curled up in my womb.' Oh, believe me, I jumped with joy,

hugged her, somersaulted on the sand. We began to make ready
for the baby, wove a crib from willow and lined it with sheep's wool.
Month by month as her body plumped my wife grew more beautiful.

Don't think me a fool, my eyes still fill with tears whenever I picture
the evening she put my hand against her stomach and I felt
our child move. But all too soon came that morning high on a hill.

We were picking herbs growing on its reddish earth but she ran ahead
to look at a strange bush with purple florets. As she touched it,
scree avalanched. Shouting, I ran like the wind but the ground opened

as if it was a mouth, swallowed her and snapped shut. Desperate,
I tried to dig with my hands and sharp stones into the soil
under the choking dust but it was hard as the marble floor in a palace.

Mad with grief, I banged my head on the earth, begged it to part
its jaws, take me too. Not a crumb of soil moved and the purple bush
had vanished – I was sure the gods had planted it to entice her.

Bellowing until I was hoarse, I searched for my beloved – the scent,
the song of her – through the heat of afternoon and all the cool night
even though I knew that I had lost her to the gods for ever.

Picture me, if you will, at dawn limping back to the cave where I found
our goats all huddled together. One bleated as if pleased to see me
and I buried my face in its flank. Inside, I grabbed the crib we'd made

and, letting out a howl, slammed it against the wall, ripped it to pieces.
Then I gulped water from the nearly empty pot to soothe my throat
but spat it out, snarling at death to take me. Wrapping myself

in a robe Arminta had made, I threw myself down. Outside an animal
moaned but I was so sunk in misery I didn't go to see if it was hurt.
Darkness was crawling into the cave when I heard a slight movement.

Half-hoping, I jumped up – it was only a moth fluttering but then I saw
my mother gliding towards me. 'The earth snatched her,' I gasped,
'and the baby. I can't live without her'. 'You can and you must.'

Pasiphae was so severe I was shocked into silence: 'You've seen
how people turn on someone not entirely human. You've been guarded
by the gods but think what your child might suffer and later generations

who are half or more than half animal. Your grief will lessen slowly.
Arminta's safe in Hades and she'll be in your dreams. Treasure
the memory of every joyful month, every year you've lived with her.

Think of my life. I'm an obedient wife but Minos has always taken
pretty girls to his bed. To him I'm simply a possession to make use of
now and then – he has as much kindness as a dry well has water.

The gods inspired my passion for the sacred bull but I must tell you
it wasn't blind passion. When I saw him browsing in a field he looked up
at me with such compassion I knew he recognized my plight.

I stood there spellbound, remembered him padding up the beach,
flanks white as foam. On our one glorious night of coupling I knew
a love, a togetherness I'd never encountered before. Needless to say

Minos had the bull transported to a place far away to make sure
there was no further union. My dear son, since then, you have been
my source of joy, you have staunched my sadness.' I knelt at her feet

and sobbed. She rocked me as she used to when I was a child,
said: 'I bring you a message from Jove: Son of the sacred bull
you are now invisible, you will cross oceans, outlive generations.'

'I want to stay near you, mother,' I begged but she stroked my horns,
put a finger on my lips, then dissolved into the night. It was noon
when I found myself outside the cave. I rounded up the goats –

what else could I do? – and with crying in my head, with my heart
in pieces, I drove the bleating animals down to the valley, left them
for men to find. Since then I've travelled through countless centuries,

visited lands of snow, scorching dust, dense forest, seen buildings
tall as hills, inventions stranger than magic: medicines which cure
deadly diseases, machines that fly like huge birds across the sky,

machines full of words and pictures. I've heard the music
of many instruments playing together, music so marvellous
it lifted me out of my body. What saddens me is that the world

is still ruled by tyrants who are as greedy and cruel as Minos.
Sometimes my dear one comes to me in the night. The scent
of her is sweet but her visits are such faint echoes of the life we shared.

Oh you, who have listened to my words, it's unburdened me
to tell you my story but I am tired of living now. I beg the gods
to lead me to Arminta in the underworld and let me drift into sleep.

ACKNOWLEDGEMENTS

Ambit, Acumen, ARTEMISpoetry, Brittle Star, The Bow-Wow Shop, Dream Catcher, Equinox, Fourteen, The French Literary Review, Hearing Voices, Iota, The London Grip, The Long Poem Magazine, Lyrical Beats (Rhythm and Muse), *Menu of Poems for All Ireland Day* (Arts and Health Partnership 2011), *The North, Poetry Ireland, Poetry Review, Quadrant* (Australia), *Scintilla, Seductive Harmonies* (Avalanche Press), *Staple, What Women Want.*

'Kaleidoscope' was the title poem in an anthology of sequences published by Cinnamon Press in 2011.

I would also like to thank the following people:

Erwin Schneider who continues to accept that I am a compulsive writer and gives me an enormous amount of practical and emotional support; John Killick who for over thirty years has given me feedback on poems as I write them; Dilys Wood for her belief in my work and her help in organizing this book, Mimi Khalvati for her rigorous, insightful and generous criticism, Caroline Price for her detailed comments on a number of poems in their later stages, the N7 workshop for helpful feedback; Stephen Stuart-Smith, my poetry publisher since 1994, for believing in my work and for all his support and consideration, Les Murray for his interest in my work and for publishing so many of my poems in *Quadrant* during the last twenty years.